Mortgage Loan Fraud Connections with Other Financial Crime:

An Evaluation of Suspicious Activity Reports Filed By Money Services Businesses, Securities and Futures Firms, Insurance Companies and Casinos

March 2009

Mortgage Loan Fraud Connections with Other Financial Crime:

An Evaluation of Suspicious Activity Reports Filed By Money Services Businesses, Securities and Futures Firms, Insurance Companies and Casinos

Office of Law Enforcement Support
Financial Crimes Enforcement Network

March 2009

Table of Contents

Executive Summary iv

Introduction 1

    Purpose and Methodology 2

Trends in Mortgage Loan Fraud Activity Reported in SAR-DIs 4

Suspicious Activity Trends Associated with Study Subjects 6

Types of Suspicious Activity Associated with Study Subjects 7

    Review of SARs filed by Money Services Businesses 7

        Wire Transfers to Foreign Countries Reported in SAR-MSBs 8

        Study Subjects Wiring Money to Nigeria 9

        Suspicious Use of Electronic Payment Systems Reported
        in SAR-MSBs 11

    Review of SARs filed by Securities and Futures Industries 11

        Suspected Securities Fraud Reported in SAR-SFs 12

        Suspected Money Laundering and Structuring Reported
        in SAR-SFs 13

        Suspected Mortgage Loan Fraud Reported in SAR-SFs 14

    Review of SARs filed by Casinos and Card Clubs 14

        Suspected Money Laundering and Structuring Reported
        in SAR-Cs 14

        Suspected Check Fraud Reported in SAR-Cs 16

Occupations of Study Subjects 17

Study Subjects in Broader BSA Reporting 19

Conclusion 21

List of Figures and Tables

List of Figures

Figure 1 – Process of Identifying Study Subjects Associated with Suspicious Activity............3

Figure 2 – Number of MLF SAR-DI Filings compared to Percent of
MLF SAR-DIs Reporting Current MLF Activity...4

Figure 3 – SAR-MSBs Reporting Study Subject Activities..6

List of Tables

Table 1 – Activities of Study Subjects Reported in SAR-MSBs.................................8

Table 2 – Foreign Countries Named in SAR-MSB Narrative Reports...........................9

Table 3 – Activities of Study Subjects Reported in SAR-SFs.................................12

Table 4 – Activities of Study Subjects Reported in SAR-Cs..................................15

Table 5 – MLF Subjects Identified in BSA Reports Cross-referenced..........................20

Executive Summary

The purpose of this study is to better understand the relationship between mortgage loan fraud and other financial crime and to identify ways in which financial crime extends through multiple financial industries. Previous Financial Crimes Enforcement Network (FinCEN) studies have identified general trends and patterns in Suspicious Activity Reports (SARs) that documented suspected mortgage loan fraud. This study examines the activities of a group of individuals and organizations reported in depository institution SARs (SAR-DIs) for suspected mortgage loan fraud ("MLF subjects") and identifies patterns of activities associated with these MLF subjects by evaluating three other types of SARs: those filed by money services businesses (SAR-MSBs); securities brokers, securities dealers, or insurance companies (SAR-SFs); and casinos or card clubs (SAR-Cs).

Examining a 5-year period, from July 2003 through June 2008, FinCEN identified approximately 156,000 MLF subjects reported by depository institutions in SAR-DIs. Approximately 2,360 of these MLF subjects were reported for suspicious activity in 3,680 of the other SAR types. Collectively, these reports provided information about ways in which the MLF subjects and associated subjects reportedly hid, moved, or disposed of large sums of cash. They also provided information about other suspected financial crime involving MLF subjects, such as stock manipulation, insurance fraud, check fraud, and fraudulent casino transactions.

Suspicious activities of MLF subjects most often reported in the SAR types reviewed were money laundering and transactions apparently structured to avoid currency transaction reporting requirements, accounting for 85 percent of SAR-MSBs, 47 percent of SAR-Cs, and 28 percent of SAR-SFs.

Filers of SAR-Cs reported check fraud by MLF subjects at a significantly higher rate than check fraud by the total population reported in all SAR-Cs. Check fraud was reported in 17 percent of SAR-Cs reporting MLF subjects, compared to 3 percent of all SAR-Cs for the same 5-year period.

SAR-MSB filers reported in 23 percent of reports that MLF subjects attempted to conceal or alter their identities. Many of these subjects wired payments to as many as ten mortgage lending companies in a single day, suggesting that some MLF subjects maintained loans for multiple straw buyers and attempted to conceal from the lenders that mortgage payments were not paid by the straw buyers.

Approximately 70 percent of SAR-MSBs described suspicious wire transfers by MLF subjects, and 34 percent described wire transfers by MLF subjects to foreign countries. Nigeria was the most frequently reported foreign destination of funds, representing

10 percent of MLF subject activity reported in SAR-MSBs. In contrast, wire transfers to Nigeria reported in all SAR-MSBs represented only 3 percent of activity reported. A review of SAR-DIs filed on MLF subjects who wired funds to Nigeria showed that 76 percent of these subjects were reported as borrowers in a fraudulent mortgage scheme.

Securities fraud was identified in 23 percent of SAR-SFs reporting MLF subjects, compared to 16 percent of all SAR-SFs in the same 5-year period. SAR-SF reports of study subjects presenting suspicious documents or identification were unusually high – 15 percent of study subject SAR-SFs, compared to 6 percent of all SAR-SFs. Also, SAR-SF filers reported a higher incidence of identity theft by MLF subjects from July 2007 through June 2008 than in the previous four years combined.

Professionals in real estate and financial industries frequently were reported as subjects in all of the SARs examined for this report, particularly in SAR-MSBs and SAR-SFs. This finding is consistent with findings in a previous FinCEN mortgage loan fraud report that real estate and financial industry insiders were frequently named in mortgage loan fraud SARs. Financial industry occupations, including mortgage broker, stock broker, insurance agent, and certified public accountant, were documented in 32 percent of the SAR-SFs reviewed. Twenty-one percent of subjects were identified in SAR-SFs as real estate professionals, such as real estate agent, real estate developer, property manager, appraiser, and title agent. Similarly, real estate and financial occupations constituted the largest occupation groups reported on SAR-MSBs.

In addition to the three types of SARs reviewed in this study, other BSA reports contain a significant volume of information on MLF subjects. Of the 156,000 MLF subjects reported in SAR-DIs for mortgage loan fraud in the 5-year period studied, 230 were reported for transactions in Reports of International Transportation of Currency or Monetary Instruments (CMIRs) and 1,220 were reported in Reports of Cash Payments Over $10,000 Received in a Trade or Business (Forms 8300) for the same period. MLF subjects also were named in approximately 23,000 SAR-DIs that reported suspicious activity other than mortgage loan fraud. These SAR-DIs documented suspected structuring and money laundering, as well as check fraud, consumer loan fraud, credit card fraud, identity theft, and wire fraud.

FinCEN studies of mortgage loan fraud published in 2006, 2008, and 2009, have indicated that depository institutions filed increasingly large numbers of SAR-DIs reporting suspected mortgage loan fraud from 1996 to mid-2008. However, since mortgage loan fraud SAR-DIs often identify suspicious activities that occurred a year or more before the report is filed, trends in mortgage loan fraud SAR-DI filings can be different from trends in the underlying mortgage loan fraud activity. This study identified reported mortgage loan fraud activity over a 5-year period and found that the percentage of SAR-DIs filed between July 2007 and June 2008 that reported mortgage loan fraud occurring in the same 12-month period was 37 percent, compared to 49 percent in the previous 12-month period. In addition, the percentage of current mortgage loan fraud reported between July 2006 and June 2007 was less than in the previous 12-month period. Therefore, as the number of newly filed SAR-DIs reporting mortgage loan fraud increased from July 2006 through June 2008, the proportion of those SAR-DIs reporting current mortgage loan fraud activity decreased by more than 28 percent.

Introduction

Mortgage loan fraud involves intentional misrepresentations to a lender for the purpose of obtaining a loan that would otherwise not be advanced by the lender. The most egregious form of mortgage loan fraud, referred to as fraud for profit, typically involves one or more of the following: a grossly inflated appraisal, first and second position mortgage loans financing 100 percent of the alleged property value, and material misrepresentations on the loan application, such as inflated income, false deposit balances, and omitted debt disclosures. A borrower in a mortgage loan fraud for profit scheme who is acting as a straw buyer typically claims an intention to live in the house as a primary residence but rarely moves in or even looks at the property. A so-called investor may coordinate multiple purchases with multiple straw buyers with the intention of flipping each property to a new straw buyer within a year. The motivation for mortgage loan fraud for profit is money, which may be shared by the investor, the mortgage broker who arranges for financing through a lender, the title agent who processes the title transfer and loan disbursement, the appraiser, and the straw buyer who effectively sells the use of his name and credit to acquire the loan.

Some mortgage loan fraud is reported through Suspicious Activity Reports (SARs) required under the Bank Secrecy Act (BSA). Original and acquiring mortgage lenders may file SARs documenting suspicions of mortgage loan fraud based on irregularities identified in loan documentation. Some mortgage lenders do not file SARs, because they are not directly subject to BSA rules.

BSA reports alone cannot be used to track proceeds of criminal activity or determine relationships among activities with any precise degree of confidence. Therefore, the aim of this study is not to track proceeds of mortgage loan fraud. Rather, this study seeks to identify and describe a collection of activities that are attributable to a set of subjects suspected of mortgage loan fraud some time between mid-2003 and mid-2008. The activities examined are primarily those reported by securities firms, insurance companies, casinos, and businesses that offer check cashing, money transfer, and money order services.

This report offers an overview of SAR filings by non-depository institutions associated with mortgage loan fraud by virtue of their connection to subjects named by depository institutions in SAR filings for suspected mortgage loan fraud ("MLF subjects") to assist regulators and other stakeholders in assessing patterns and trends of financial crime that may be associated with mortgage loan fraud. FinCEN will continue discussions with its regulatory, law enforcement, and industry partners on how SAR data may enhance analysis of broad mortgage fraud issues. These discussions may provide additional insights into the significance of, for example, changes in the volume of certain types of reports, associations among certain reported activities, and the effectiveness of anti-fraud and anti-money laundering (AML) measures.

For depository institutions, this report provides further context in the experiences across the financial industry as a whole. The analysis builds upon FinCEN's earlier mortgage loan fraud reports that detailed vulnerabilities to fraud, identified different types of fraudulent activity, and identified "red flag" indicators of possible fraud. Providing such information can help financial institutions improve the efficiency and effectiveness of BSA compliance and reporting activities, identify potentially illegal activity, and share information with law enforcement in support of the investigation and prosecution of criminal activity. FinCEN specifically seeks to help financial institutions learn from the experiences of others as to ways to protect the institution and its customers from being victims of fraud. This most recent report aims to provide new insights as to how a variety of businesses besides lending institutions can play a role in the discovery of potential fraud.

Purpose and Methodology

To better understand how mortgage loan fraud may relate to other financial crime, FinCEN identified subjects reported in depository institution SARs (SAR-DIs) for suspected mortgage loan fraud and evaluated activities of these MLF subjects reported in non-depository financial institution SARs[1]: those filed by money services businesses (SAR-MSBs); securities brokers, securities dealers, or insurance companies (SAR-SFs); and casinos or card clubs (SAR-Cs).

All of the SARs discussed in this report have a common element: a depository institution reported its suspicions that the subjects were engaged in mortgage loan fraud between July 2003 and June 2008. This study focuses on analysis of suspected financial crime other than mortgage loan fraud committed by MLF subjects and reported by non-depository financial institutions. The SARs identified and evaluated in this study describe ways in which MLF subjects engaged in suspicious activity that may be related to a mortgage loan fraud scheme, such as money laundering, structuring, and fraudulent statements of income, and suspicious activity that may be unrelated to mortgage loan fraud, such as stock manipulation, insurance fraud, and check fraud.

---

1. This study specifically examined suspicious activity reported by financial institutions other than depository institutions; therefore, a comprehensive analysis of suspicious activity reported in SAR-DIs is not included in this report.

FinCEN identified approximately 162,000 SAR-DIs documenting mortgage loan fraud between July 2003 and June 2008.[2] Unique identifiers[3] of the 156,000 subjects named in the mortgage loan fraud SAR-DIs were cross-referenced with SAR-MSBs, SAR-SFs and SAR-Cs that reported suspicious activity of at least one of the MLF subjects in the same 5-year period. The resulting set of 9,008 study subjects consists of 2,360 MLF subjects and 6,648 associated subjects who were reported in SAR-MSBs, SAR-SFs, or SAR-Cs for engaging in suspicious activity between July 2003 and June 2008 (see Figure 1).

Figure 1

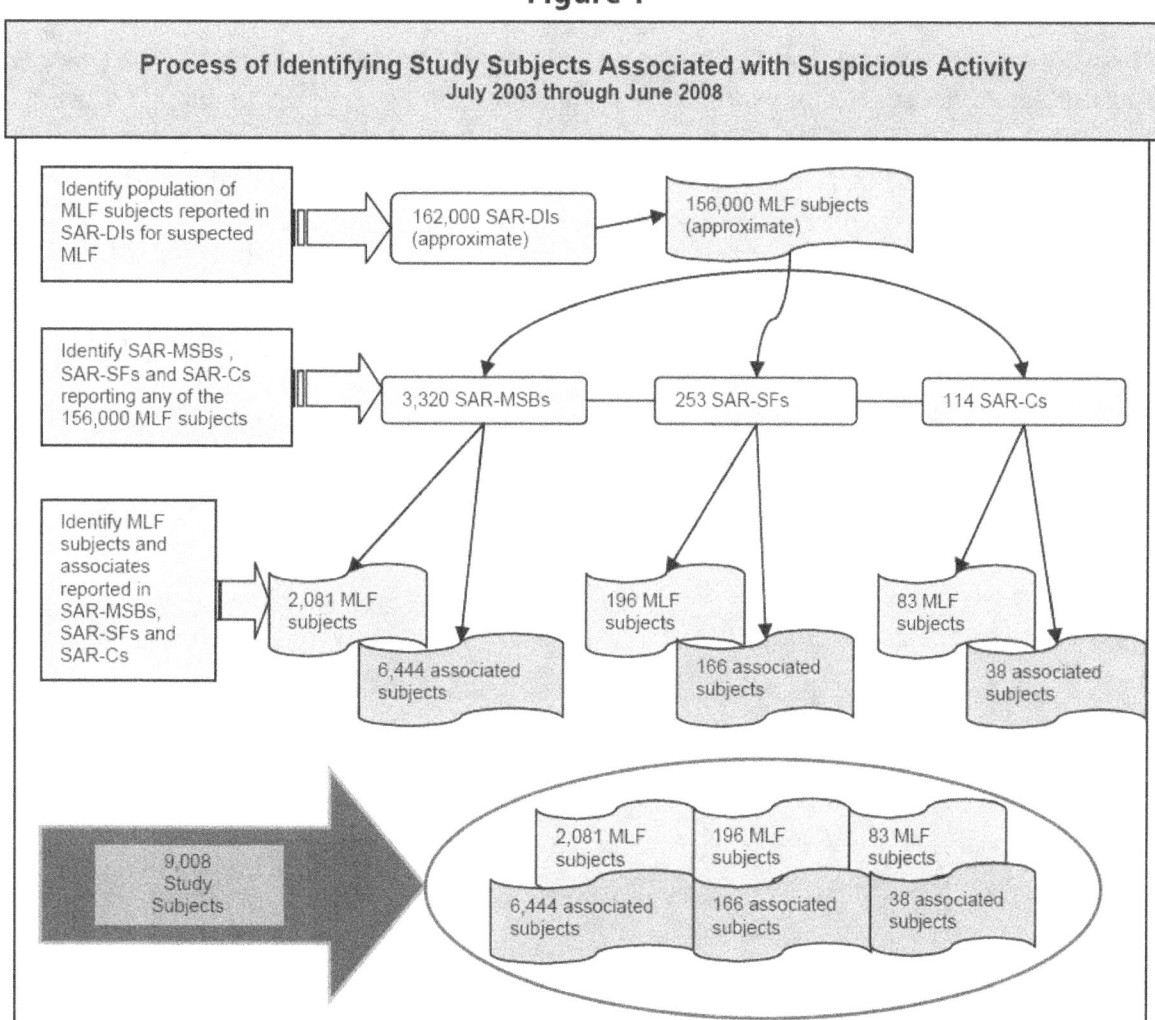

2. Activity start dates, rather than report filing dates, were used because related financial crime such as money laundering was likely to correspond with the time the MLF subject fraudulently obtained funds rather than the date a financial institution reported the mortgage loan fraud.

3. Unique identifiers, such as Social Security numbers (SSNs) and driver's license, passport, and other identifying numbers (IDs), were used rather than names to reduce the likelihood of false matches when cross referencing SAR-MSBs, SAR-SFs, and SAR-Cs. Some false data was anticipated from the use of IDs, since many IDs are only unique within the issuing jurisdiction. Therefore, IDs were only used for SAR-MSBs, which often do not include the SSNs of subjects.

Trends in Mortgage Loan Fraud Activity Reported in SAR-DIs

I n 2006, 2008, and 2009, FinCEN studies[4] found that depository institutions filed an increasingly large number of SAR-DIs documenting suspected mortgage loan fraud between 1996 and 2008. From July 2007 through June 2008, depository institutions filed more than 62,000 SAR-DIs reporting mortgage loan fraud, compared to 14,484, four years earlier. SAR-DI filing dates and dates of the underlying suspicious activity in reports of mortgage loan fraud, however, can differ significantly because financial institutions often detect and report indications of mortgage loan fraud a year or more after the activity occurs.[5] For example, a lender may review a mortgage loan file after payments are delinquent by several months and discover that the borrower purchased multiple houses simultaneously or the appraiser valued renovations that were never made. Therefore, a fraud that occurred in 2006 may be reported in 2007 or later.

Figure 2

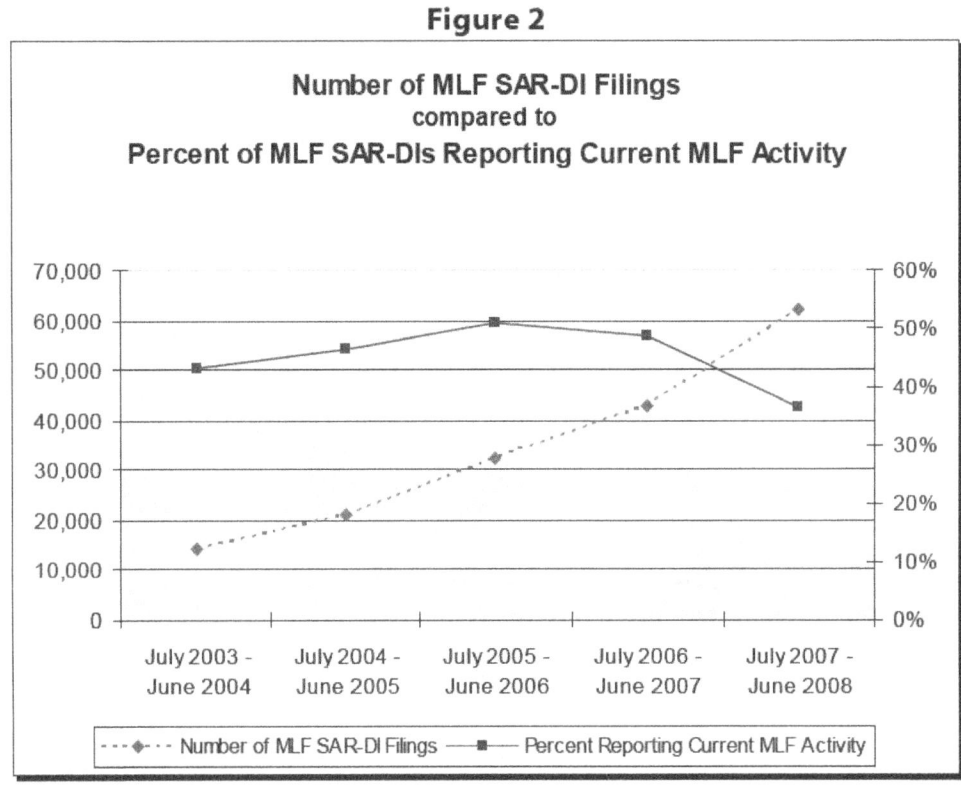

4. *Mortgage Loan Fraud: An Industry Assessment based Upon Suspicious Activity Report Analysis, November 2006;*
    Mortgage Loan Fraud: An Update of Trends Based Upon an Analysis of Suspicious Activity Reports, April 2008;
    and Filing Trends in Mortgage Loan Fraud: A Review of Suspicious Activity Reports Filed July 1, 2007 through
    June 30, 2008, February 2009.

5. Each SAR documents the date the *report was filed*. Each SAR also indicates a start date of suspected activity, which is the date the filer believes the suspicious activity began. In mortgage loan fraud SAR-DIs, the start date is often the date the loan closed and property ownership changed.

Analysis of SAR-DIs based on the dates suspicious activities began relative to the dates reports were filed indicates that the percentage of SAR-DIs filed that reported mortgage loan fraud occurring in the same 12-month period decreased beginning July 2006. For example, 37 percent of mortgage loan fraud SAR-DIs filed between July 2007 and June 2008 reported mortgage loan fraud activity during the same 12-month period, compared to 51 percent of mortgage loan fraud SAR-DIs filed between July 2005 and June 2006 (see Figure 2). In other words, the increasing number of mortgage loan fraud SARs filed by depository institutions between July 2006 and June 2008 reported proportionately less current mortgage loan fraud, year-over-year, for two years beginning mid-2006.

A relative decline in mortgage loan fraud reported in SAR-DIs over a 2-year period does not necessarily indicate a continuing decline in reported mortgage loan fraud and may not reflect a change in the actual incidence of mortgage loan fraud in the larger population of mortgage loans, some of which is not captured in BSA data. However, the change in SAR-DI reported mortgage loan fraud activity is significant and worth noting. A variety of factors could account for the change, including changes in the structure of financial institutions, ownership of mortgage loans, and policy changes.

Changes that could account for a decline in current mortgage loan fraud activity in 2007 and 2008 include reductions in Sub-prime[6] and Alt-A[7] loan originations, reductions in all mortgage loan originations,[8] increases in law enforcement actions against perpetrators of mortgage loan fraud,[9] increased public awareness of mortgage loan fraud, and improved detection of mortgage loan fraud by lenders before funds are disbursed.[10] Continued declines in real estate market values, additional foreclosures, additional job losses, new lending programs, and other factors could impact in the future the downward trend that was observed in the period studied.

---

6. Sub-prime loans are mortgage loans on less favorable terms than prime loans and have typically been extended to borrowers who do not qualify for prime loans based on their credit ratings, incomes, assets, or other debts.

7. Alt-A loans are mortgage loans made to borrowers whose credit scores suggest that they qualify for "A" credit (prime loan terms) but who provide less documentation and therefore receive loan terms less favorable than prime. Stated income loans are often Alt-A loans. Analyses by the Federal National Mortgage Association have shown that misrepresentations of income, assets, and employment are significantly greater in Alt-A loans than in all other types of mortgage loans.

8. The Mortgage Bankers Association has reported declines in mortgage loan originations from 2003 through 2008 and estimated continuing declines through 2009. See www.mortgagebankers.org/newsandmedia/presscenter.

9. See the 2007 FBI report on mortgage fraud at www.fbi.gov/publications/fraud/mortgage_fraud07.htm.

10. Mortgage loan fraud analyses released by FinCEN in April 2008 and February 2009 reported increases in the percentage of SAR-DIs filed prior to loan approval or disbursement.

Suspicious Activity Trends Associated with Study Subjects

S AR-MSB filers reported a significantly larger number of study subjects for suspicious activity than did filers of SAR-SFs or SAR-Cs. SAR-MSB filers reported that study subject activity increased between July 2003 and June 2005, remained high from 2005 through 2006, and declined beginning in 2007 (see Figure 3). The similarity between current-period mortgage loan fraud trends reported in SAR-DIs and study subject activity reported in SAR-MSBs suggests that some study subjects may have used cash obtained from fraudulent mortgage loans to wire funds or purchase money orders in an effort to launder illegally obtained funds.

Figure 3

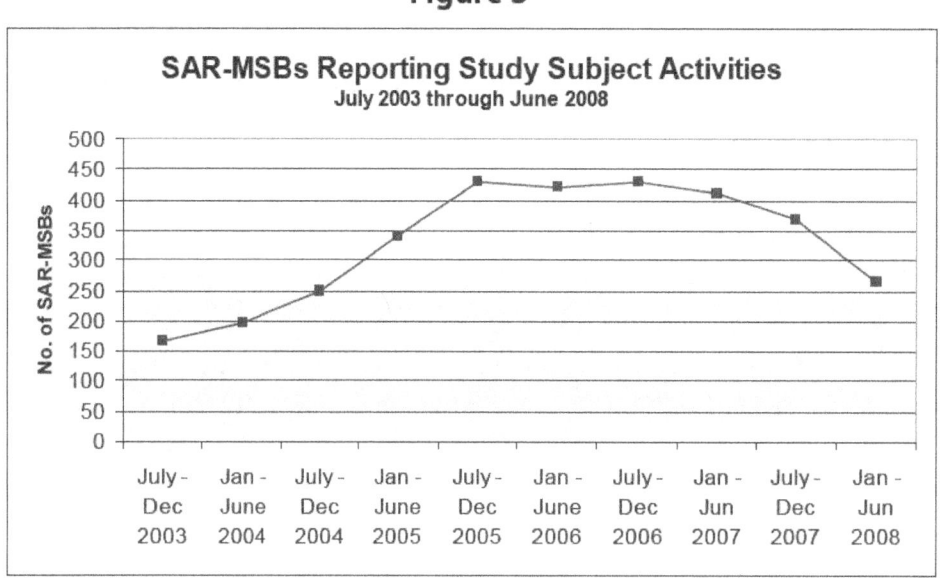

In contrast, study subject activity reported in SAR-SFs continued to increase in 2007 and 2008, with the greatest number of activities occurring between July 2007 and June 2008. Analysis of activities revealed that the largest contributor to the increase in study subject activity from July 2007 through June 2008 was reported identity theft, which increased from eight reported incidents between July 2006 and June 2007 to 67 reported incidents between July 2007 and June 2008.

Filers of SAR-Cs reported more suspicious casino activities by study subjects from July 2006 through June 2008 than in the previous three years. Beginning July 2007 and continuing through June 2008, casinos reported a significant increase in structuring activity by study subjects. Suspected structuring comprised 57 percent of study subject activity reported in SAR-Cs in the first half of 2008, compared to 33 percent in the first half of 2007 and 17 percent in the first half of 2006.

Types of Suspicious Activity Associated with Study Subjects

F ilers of SAR-MSBs, SAR-SFs and SAR-Cs who reported study subject activities cited structuring and money laundering more frequently than any other suspicious activities, reporting study subjects for structuring or money laundering in 85 percent of SAR-MSBs, 47 percent of SAR-Cs, and 28 percent of SAR-SFs. Approximately 13 percent of the reviewed SAR-MSBs reported subjects sending electronic payments to multiple lenders in a single day. Nearly 10 percent of the SAR-MSBs reported subjects wiring money to Nigeria – a significantly larger percentage of Nigerian-related activity than is typically reported in SAR-MSBs.[11] Securities fraud, including market manipulation, insider trading and fictitious trading, was reported in 23 percent of the SAR-SFs reviewed. Check fraud was reported in 16 percent of the SAR-SFs reviewed and 17 percent of the SAR-Cs reviewed. Mortgage loan fraud was identified as a suspicious activity in 11 percent of the SAR-SFs reviewed.[12]

Review of SARs filed by Money Services Businesses

SAR-MSBs are filed by businesses that operate as money transmitters, check cashers, or sellers of money orders or traveler's checks. Filers of SAR-MSBs that reported study subject activities identified suspected structuring or money laundering in over 85 percent of reports. The most common structuring method, cited in 25 percent of reports, was two or more study subjects apparently working together to transfer or receive funds in amounts below reporting requirements. Reported activities of study subjects that were proportionately high, compared to activities of all SAR-MSBs, were (1) altering transaction amounts to avoid currency transaction reporting and (2) using false identification cards or documents (see Table 1).

---

11. Information about wire transfers to Nigeria is based on a sample of study subject SAR-MSBs consisting of 808 randomly selected reports and is representative of the SAR-MSB study population with respect to foreign countries named in the narrative.

12. Although the SAR-SFs reviewed were all associated with MLF subjects, the filers of SAR-SFs may have no information regarding a MLF subject's participation in mortgage loan fraud at the time of the SAR-SF filing.

Table 1

Activities of Study Subjects Most Frequently Reported in SAR-MSBs Compared to Activity Reported in All SAR-MSBs July 2003 through June 2008			
Activity Category	**Percent of Study Subject SAR-MSBs**	**VS**	**Percent of All SAR-MSBs**
Frequent Purchase Under $3,000	27.38%		35.68%
Alter to Avoid Recordkeeping	25.66%		35.24%
Two Individuals Working Together	25.09%		19.23%
Alter to Avoid Currency Transaction Reports	17.83%		11.18%
Multiple Locations in a Short Time	10.81%		12.58%
Multiple or False IDs	9.22%		2.93%
Two Individuals Using the Same ID	3.73%		1.19%
Changes in Name	1.84%		4.00%
Bribe as a Tip or Gratuity	0.12%		0.15%
Percentages may not total 100 percent because SARs may report multiple activity categories or include no activity description.			

Approximately 70 percent of the SAR-MSBs reviewed described suspicious wire transfers of funds; 23 percent described attempts to conceal identity using name variations, false identification documents, or multiple addresses; and 13 percent described suspicious use of electronic payment systems.

Wire Transfers to Foreign Countries Reported in SAR-MSBs

Nearly half (48 percent) of SAR-MSBs that reported suspicious wire transfers by study subjects indicated that funds were wired to foreign countries. SAR-MSB filers reported that senders or receivers demonstrated some form of deceptive behavior by providing false or conflicting identification, multiple addresses or inconsistent phone numbers in 24 percent of the narratives describing wire transfers to foreign countries. This type of deceptive behavior is typically associated with money laundering activity.

Suspicious activity associated with Nigeria was reported in SAR-MSB narrative reports more often than any other foreign country, followed by China and Mexico. Approximately 10 percent of the SAR-MSBs reviewed indicated that subjects wired money to Nigeria. In contrast, Nigeria was named in only 3 percent of the total population of SAR-MSBs. The total amount of money reported by SAR-MSBs associated with both study subjects and Nigeria was $6.3 million. Table 2 shows the frequency with which foreign countries are named in sampled SAR-MSBs involving study subjects versus all SAR-MSBs filed from July 2003 through June 2008.

Table 2

Foreign Countries Named in SAR-MSB Narrative Reports Sampled SAR-MSBs vs All SAR-MSBs July 2003 through June 2008				
Foreign Country Receiving Wire Transfers	**Percent of SAR-MSBs Naming Study Subjects**	**VS**	**Foreign Country Named in SAR-MSB Narratives**	**Percent of All SAR-MSBs**
Nigeria	9.78%		Nigeria	3.32%
China	8.29%		China	6.98%
Mexico	6.56%		Mexico	7.55%
Philippines	3.22%		Philippines	1.12%
Costa Rica	2.10%		Costa Rica	0.92%
Nicaragua	1.73%		Nicaragua	0.70%
United Kingdom	1.73%		United Kingdom	0.11%
Guatemala	1.36%		Guatemala	1.72%
Ghana	1.24%		Ghana	0.46%
Panama	1.24%		Panama	0.77%

Study Subjects Wiring Money to Nigeria

The sampled study subjects who were reported in SAR-MSBs for wiring money to Nigeria were examined as a unique group, given the atypical frequency of wire transfers to Nigeria. A review of the SAR-DIs filed on these subjects revealed reports of suspected structuring, money laundering, and check fraud, in addition to mortgage loan fraud.

The total amount of money reported in the SAR-DIs indicating suspicions of mortgage loan fraud by study subjects who wired money to Nigeria was about $15 million. Most (76 percent) of these subjects were mortgage loan borrowers with likely roles as straw buyers, typically receiving $10,000 to $20,000 per mortgage loan fraud transaction from a third party.[13] Some of the borrowers were reported as property owners who initiated

---

13. Anecdotal reports from law enforcement indicate that straw buyers frequently receive cash payments of at least $10,000 to entice them to sign mortgage loan documents for property they have no intention of occupying or maintaining. This payment is typically provided by a third party for use of the straw buyer's name and good credit.

fraudulent home equity lines of credit or refinanced existing mortgage loans. Of the borrowers with documented occupations, 25 percent were in the construction business, 25 percent were in a services business, 16 percent were real estate agents, and 16 percent worked in sales positions (which may include real estate sales). Thirty percent of the mortgage loan fraud SAR-DIs reported misrepresentations of income, assets, and debts on mortgage loan applications. A number of SAR-DI filers indicated that subjects used stated loan applications, which typically require no proof of income and no verification of debt. Some filers stated that they would not have funded the loans if the borrowers had reported their true income or disclosed loans on other property.

Structured withdrawals were reported in 13 percent of the SAR-DIs and accounted for $1.8 million in activity. SAR-DI filers reported study subjects who made numerous cash withdrawals in increments below $10,000 on the same day or within days of one another. Money laundering was suspected in 10 percent of the SAR-DIs, accounting for an additional $1.4 million of activity. One SAR-DI filer reported that $300,000 was wired by a study subject to businesses and individuals located in Africa, Asia, and Europe. Another report documented large sums of money deposited into an account owned by a relative of a convicted mortgage fraud felon. A SAR-DI filer reporting both mortgage loan fraud and structuring described a study subject in the construction business who placed a construction lien against a property after fraudulently recording the true mortgage as discharged. The subject deposited proceeds from a loan against the construction lien and then structured withdrawals from his account. Twenty percent of the study subjects who structured withdrawals were in sales occupations, 19 percent were mortgage brokers, and 19 percent were in construction occupations.

Approximately 28 percent of SAR-DIs reviewed reported $1.2 million in check fraud activity, together with or independent of mortgage loan fraud, money laundering, and structuring. Approximately 22 percent of the SAR-DIs reviewed reported that study subjects deposited or made loan payments with counterfeit checks or checks that were returned unpaid. One subject made a $210,000 payment on his existing home equity line of credit using a worthless check, accessed the newly available credit, and wired the full amount to a location in Asia. Another subject deposited a counterfeit check for $50,000 and then requested a $30,000 wire to an individual in Asia. A week later, the same subject deposited a counterfeit check for $55,000. Another subject repeatedly participated in activities that appeared to be scams, depositing counterfeit checks into his account, wiring money to a location in Africa, and discussing with bank employees profits anticipated from an online arrangement that never materialized.

Suspicious Use of Electronic Payment Systems Reported in SAR-MSBs

Suspicious use of electronic payment systems was reported in 13 percent of the SAR-MSBs associated with study subjects. Filers reported that study subjects frequently sent electronic mortgage loan payments to as many as ten mortgage companies on the same day. SAR-MSB filers also reported that study subjects who sent electronic mortgage payments frequently used multiple addresses, multiple identification numbers, name variations, and conflicting telephone numbers. This activity is consistent with efforts by so-called mortgage loan fraud investors[14] to make lenders believe that the borrower, or straw buyer, maintains the loan payments; to conceal the identity of the investor; and to launder funds obtained illegally. Lending institutions have characterized this kind of activity as a tactic designed to avoid a lender review of mortgage loan documents based on loan payment delinquencies in the first year following a loan disbursement.

Review of SARs filed by Securities and Futures Industries

During the study period, July 2003 through June 2008, SAR-SFs were filed by businesses that operate as securities brokers, securities dealers, or insurance companies. SAR-SFs that named study subjects reported a variety of suspicious activities including money laundering, structuring, securities fraud, check fraud, wire fraud, forgery, and identity theft. Compared to all SAR-SFs for the period July 2003 through June 2008, reports of study subjects presenting suspicious documents or suspicious identification were unusually high – 15 percent of study subject SAR-SFs, compared to 6 percent of all SAR-SFs (see Table 3).

---

14. The term mortgage loan fraud investor is used here to mean someone who orchestrates a mortgage loan fraud for the purpose of "skimming" equity from a mortgage loan based on a fraudulently inflated appraisal or other fraudulent documents.

Table 3

Activities of Study Subjects Most Frequently Reported in SAR-SFs Compared to Activity Reported in All SAR-SFs July 2003 through June 2008			
Activity Category	**Percent of Study Subject SAR-SFs**	**VS**	**Percent of All SAR-SFs**
Other	38.74%		32.28%
Money Laundering or Structuring	28.06%		28.80%
Securities Fraud (combined category)	22.53%		15.93%
Significant Suspicious Transaction	17.00%		12.86%
Check Fraud	15.81%		11.14%
Suspicious Documents or Identification	14.62%		5.76%
Wire Fraud	12.25%		12.18%
Forgery	8.70%		3.21%
Embezzlement or Theft of Funds	7.91%		6.49%
ID Theft	7.11%		15.12%
Mail Fraud	2.37%		2.82%
Percentages may not total 100 percent because SARs may report multiple activity categories or include no activity description.			

Most account activity reported by SAR-SF filers involved incoming funds, with 25 percent deposited as checks and 19 percent entering accounts by wire transfer. Most funds coming into and going out study subject accounts originated from or were sent to domestic locations. Filers of SAR-SFs identified mortgage loan fraud-related activities in 11 percent of the reports, describing activities such as requests for verification of brokerage account balances.

A small number of MLF subjects reportedly participated in a relatively large percentage of the suspicious activity reported in the SAR-SFs reviewed. Four MLF subjects were reported for 15 percent of the suspicious activity documented in the SAR-SFs. The total transaction amount reported for these four subjects was approximately $92.7 million.

Suspected Securities Fraud Reported in SAR-SFs

Securities fraud was identified in 23 percent of the SAR-SFs that reported suspicious activity by study subjects, compared to 16 percent of all SAR-SFs during the same 5-year period. The category "securities fraud," for purposes of this report, includes market manipulation, insider trading, fictitious trading, and other securities fraud. FinCEN's 2008 report on mortgage loan fraud identified California as the state that reported mortgage loan fraud most frequently.[15] A review of SAR-MSBs and SAR-Cs also showed that most study subjects resided in California. A review of SAR-SFs, however, showed more suspicious activity by residents of Florida than any other state, including California.

Analysis of the Florida activity reported in SAR-SFs showed that 46 percent of the Florida data represented activities of one MLF subject and his associates. From 2004 through 2007, this subject deposited millions of shares of penny stocks into four brokerage accounts. Then, with the help of more than 20 associates, the subject sold and repurchased the stocks, moving money and stocks through dozens of accounts and generating between $1.5 and $7.5 million each year. This kind of activity suggests that the subject and his associates engaged in pre-arranged trading, buying and selling stocks from one another and incrementally manipulating the stock price upward. In 2007, the subject transferred a large block of stock to a mortgage broker, who subsequently prepared a fraudulent loan application in the subject's name. The subject also transferred large blocks of stocks to mortgage lenders, property developers, and attorneys.

Suspected Money Laundering and Structuring Reported in SAR-SFs

More than one-quarter (28 percent) of the SAR-SFs reporting study subjects pertained to structuring or money laundering activities. Thirty-seven percent of these reports described structuring activities in which a subject systematically deposited or withdrew funds in small increments, apparently to avoid BSA currency transaction reporting requirements. Seventeen percent of these reports, many of which were filed by insurance companies, described purchases or unusual restructuring of insurance products indicative of money laundering. For example, one subject converted a term life insurance policy with an annual premium of $2,000 into two whole life insurance policies with annual premiums totaling $100,000. Premium payments for the new policies were made with personal checks, corporate checks, and cash. Since whole life policies typically have cash value that is related to deposits and premiums made to the policy, and that cash value is liquid, or accessible to the policy holder immediately or in the near term, whole life policies can be used to hide money or launder illegal assets. Term life policies, on the other hand, have no value until the policy holder dies, so they are only useful as a money laundering tool if the policy holder wishes to pass illegally obtained funds to the beneficiaries of the policy.

---

15. *Mortgage Loan Fraud: An Update of Trends Based Upon an Analysis of Suspicious Activity Reports,* April 2008.

Suspected Mortgage Loan Fraud Reported in SAR-SFs

Some reports categorized by SAR-SF filers only as "other" identified accounts belonging to subjects of pending investigations or legal actions and described no account activity that was suspicious. Suspected mortgage loan fraud activity, including submission of fraudulent deposit verification forms, was also classified as "other" because the category "mortgage fraud" is not included as a suspicious activity classification on the SAR-SF form. Mortgage loan fraud activity, identified in SAR-SFs through a review of report narratives, was described in 11 percent of the SAR-SFs. Half of these reports pertained to fraudulent requests for verification of assets or deposits. Mortgage brokers reportedly made these requests to increase incomes of prospective borrowers who were applying for mortgage loans for which they would otherwise have been unqualified. In all cases, the requests were altered or otherwise falsified. For example, verification forms listed fictitious assets or combined non-customer or fictitious names with existing customer account information.

Review of SARs filed by Casinos and Card Clubs

Structuring accounted for approximately 45 percent of SAR-Cs reporting study subjects. Filers of SAR-Cs reported subjects for structuring casino transactions by making small, incremental payments on markers,[16] and using multiple casino agents to cash in casino chips in increments below the threshold for cash transaction reporting. Compared to all SAR-Cs reporting activity between July 2003 and June 2008, reports of check fraud by study subjects were unusually high – 17 percent of study subject SAR-Cs, compared to 3 percent of all SAR-Cs. Activities classified as "other" on SAR-C forms accounted for 18 percent of suspicious activity reported. Activities that filers most frequently classified as "other" were minimal gaming with large transactions, refusal to provide identification, and production of false identification (see Table 4).

A small number of MLF subjects reportedly participated in a relatively large percentage of the suspicious activity reported in the SAR-Cs reviewed. Five MLF subjects were reported for 20 percent of the activity documented in the SAR-Cs reviewed. The total transaction amount reported for these five subjects was approximately $2.1 million.

Suspected Money Laundering and Structuring Reported in SAR-Cs

Filers of SAR-Cs reported a variety of behaviors that may indicate money laundering activity by study subjects. For example, filers reported some study subjects for writing checks or sending wire transfers to casino employees. The casino employees then

---

16. A marker is a type of casino loan that allows a gambler to receive chips at a table and pay the casino later.

withdrew cash from their accounts and returned the money to the subjects. Casino employees typically received $80 in cash as a "tip" for each transaction. One casino employee conducted at least 60 of these transactions in one year. Some study subjects requested casino markers and then repaid the markers in small increments of cash. These subjects participated in minimal or no gaming. This technique may be a money laundering method used to place illegally obtained money into the legitimate financial system.

Table 4

Activities of Study Subjects Most Frequently Reported in SAR-Cs Compared to Activity Reported in All SAR-Cs July 2003 through June 2008			
Activity Category	**Percent of Study Subject SAR-Cs**	**VS**	**Percent of All SAR-Cs**
Structuring	44.74%		39.72%
Other	18.42%		26.42%
Check Fraud	16.67%		3.27%
Minimal Gaming with Large Transactions	11.40%		19.77%
Unusual Use of Counter Checks or Markers	7.02%		3.06%
False or Conflicting Identification	4.39%		9.52%
Unusual Use of Negotiable Instruments	4.39%		2.43%
No Apparent Business or Lawful Purpose	3.51%		6.04%
Money Laundering	2.63%		4.27%
Bribery	1.75%		0.27%
Unusual Use of Wire Transfers	1.75%		0.84%
Large U.S. Currency Exchange	0.88%		4.56%
Embezzlement or Theft	0.88%		0.44%
Percentages may not total 100 percent because SARs may report multiple activity categories or include no activity description.			

SAR-Cs reported study subjects who inserted currency into slot machines and received Tickets-In-Tickets-Out (TITOs).[17] After little or no gaming, the subjects cashed out the TITOs. This behavior may be a method of exchanging small bills for larger bills or establishing a legitimate source for illegally obtained funds. Subjects

---

17. Tickets-In-Tickets-Out (TITO) are bar-coded tickets, printed by a slot or poker machine in lieu of cash, that can be redeemed for cash or inserted for play in a TITO machine.

who exchanged small bills of the same denomination for casino chips were also reported in SAR-Cs. These subjects participated in minimal or no gaming and requested casino checks when the chips were cashed out.

Suspected Check Fraud Reported in SAR-Cs

Filers of the SAR-Cs identified a significant amount of check fraud by study subjects – 17 percent of study subject SAR-Cs compared to 3 percent of all SAR-Cs reporting activity during the same 5-year period. Filers reported study subjects who deposited fraudulent cashier's checks into casino accounts and withdrew the funds before the checks were returned unpaid and the filers became aware that the checks were fraudulent. Subjects who conducted this activity typically participated in minimal gaming. SAR-C filers also reported study subjects who filled out blank casino checks (counter checks) with their bank account information to be used as collateral against casino markers. After minimal gaming, the subjects cashed out their casino chips without repaying the markers. In each instance when the casino deposited the casino check to cover the marker, the casino discovered that the account was non-existent or funds in the account were insufficient to cover the casino check.

Occupations of Study Subjects

Not surprisingly, SAR-MSBs, SAR-SFs and SAR-Cs frequently reported that study subjects held occupations in real estate and finance industries. This finding is consistent with previous FinCEN report findings that real estate and financial industry insiders were frequently named in mortgage loan fraud SARs.

Real estate occupations were often listed in SARs as simply "real estate," which could indicate a professional affiliation, such as real estate agent, or an informal designation, such as someone who invests in property. Property managers, real estate developers, appraisers, and property title agents also were included in this category. Mortgage brokers and lenders were included in the category "finance," which also includes accountants, stock brokers, and insurance agents. Other common occupations were retail services, food services, and construction.

Twenty-nine percent of all SAR-MSBs reporting study subjects included subjects employed in real estate or finance. Nineteen percent of SAR-MSB subjects reportedly held real estate occupations. Real estate agents and real estate brokers represented nearly 84 percent of this category; real estate investors, developers, and property managers represented about 12 percent; and title companies, surveyors, and appraisers represented the remaining 4 to 5 percent. Financial industry occupations comprised 10 percent of the occupations held by study subjects reported in SAR-MSBs. Mortgage brokers and mortgage companies represented 55 percent of those reporting financial industry occupations. Bank employees and loan officers represented about 32 percent of the financial industry occupations.

Twenty-seven percent of all SAR-SFs reviewed included study subjects employed in real estate or mortgage lending fields. Most of these SAR-SFs named multiple subjects in the real estate and mortgage field. Twenty-one percent of subjects were identified in SAR-SFs as real estate professionals, such as real estate agent, real estate developer, property manager, appraiser, and real estate title agent. Thirty-two percent of the SAR-SFs reviewed reported that study subjects held financial industry occupations, including mortgage broker, stock broker, insurance representative, and tax preparer. One-third (32 percent) of this group was employed or previously employed as a stock broker or investment advisor; one-quarter (25 percent) reported employment as mortgage broker or lender; and 11 percent reported employment as an accountant or tax preparer. The latter occupation – accountant or tax preparer – was associated in some reports with fictitious or altered documentation of income or deposits used to qualify a borrower for a fraudulent mortgage loan.

Study subject occupations reported in the SAR-Cs were grouped into six general categories: retail services, finance, marketing, real estate, technology, and automotive. Retail services was the most common occupation type reported, accounting for approximately 27 percent of all occupations reported.

Study Subjects in Broader BSA Reporting

I n addition to the three types of SARs reviewed in this study, other BSA reports contain a significant volume of information on MLF subjects. Of the 156,000 MLF subjects reported in 161,000 SAR-DIs for mortgage loan fraud from July 2003 through June 2008, 230 subjects were reported for transactions in 315 Reports of International Transportation of Currency or Monetary Instruments (CMIRs) and 1,220 subjects were reported in 2,500 Reports of Cash Payments Over $10,000 Received in a Trade or Business (Forms 8300) for the same period (see Table 5).

A number of MLF subjects reported in SAR-MSBs, SAR-SFs, SAR-Cs, CMIRs, and Forms 8300 were also named in each of the other reports. Table 5 shows the frequency with which MLF subjects from each BSA report also appear as subjects in other BSA reports. For example, one or more of the 2,081 MLF subjects identified in the 3,320 SAR-MSBs studied were also named in 38 filings of Form 8300 for cash payments received in a trade or business, such as a car dealer.

MLF subjects also were named in approximately 23,000 additional SAR-DIs that reported suspicious activity other than mortgage loan fraud. These SAR-DIs primarily documented suspected structuring and money laundering. They also documented suspected check fraud, consumer loan fraud, credit card fraud, identity theft, and wire fraud by MLF subjects.

Table 5

Mortgage Loan Fraud Subjects Identified in BSA Reports Cross-referenced to Other BSA Reports July 2003 through June 2008					
Population of MLF subjects reported in MLF SAR-DIs	156,000 MLF subjects (approximate)				
Reports naming one or more of the 156,000 MLF subjects	3,320 SAR-MSBs	253 SAR-SFs	114 SAR-Cs	315 CMIRs	2,500 Forms 8300
MLF subjects named in each BSA report type	**2,081 MLF subjects**	**196 MLF subjects**	**83 MLF subjects**	**230 MLF subjects**	**1,220 MLF Subjects**
SAR-MSBs naming MLF subjects from each BSA report type	n/a	8 SAR-MSBs	4 SAR-MSBs	6 SAR-MSBs	38 SAR-MSBs
SAR-SFs naming MLF subjects from each BSA report type	8 SAR-SFs	n/a	2 SAR-SFs	1 SAR-SF	17 SAR-SFs
SAR-Cs naming MLF subjects from each BSA report type	4 SAR-Cs	2 SAR-Cs	n/a	1 SAR-C	3 SAR-Cs
CMIRs naming MLF subjects from each BSA report type	6 CMIRs	1 CMIR	1 CMIR	n/a	8 CMIRs
Forms 8300 naming MLF subjects from each BSA report type	38 Forms 8300	17 Forms 8300	3 Forms 8300	8 Forms 8300	n/a

Conclusion

As is often the case with fraud schemes, some illegal activities that are integral to mortgage loan fraud also can be used in other financial crimes. For example, mortgage loan fraud may involve falsification of documents such as loan applications, W-2 forms, drivers' licenses, credit reports, and deposit verification requests. Falsified documents can be used in check fraud, wire fraud, and securities fraud to acquire money illegally or conceal identity. Some reports in all SAR-types reviewed documented efforts by study subjects to use false names, addresses, or identification documents. SAR-SF filers reported study subjects for suspicion of identify theft more frequently between July 2007 and June 2008 than in the previous four years combined. About one-fourth of SAR-MSBs reviewed reported study subjects for using false names or identification.

Although study subjects often were reported in SAR-MSBs, SAR-SFs, and SAR-Cs for attempting to hide or move large sums of cash, some study subjects reportedly manipulated stocks or deposited fraudulent checks in an effort to make money illegally. Securities fraud – including insider trading and market manipulation – was identified in 23 percent of SAR-SFs reporting study subjects, compared to 16 percent of all SAR-SFs. SAR-SF and SAR-C filers reported study subjects for check fraud in 16 to 17 percent of reports. In contrast, during the same period, check fraud was reported in 11 percent of all SAR-SFs and in 3 percent of all SAR-Cs.

This collection of BSA reports on MLF subjects illustrates the overlap of financial crimes across a variety of financial industries. While the percentage of MLF subjects reported in SAR-MSBs, SAR-SFs, and SAR-Cs is small relative to the total MLF subjects identified in SAR-DIs (less than 2 percent), information obtained from these reports shows how BSA data can inform law enforcement investigations of mortgage loan fraud activity, particularly in cases that include money laundering, structuring, identity theft, check fraud, or wire fraud activities. Information in these reports also may be useful for broad-based analyses of mortgage loan fraud activity and related financial crime. For example, one of the findings of this study was a proportional decrease in current-period mortgage loan fraud reported in SAR-DIs over a period of two years.

Although the causes of this decrease are not known, FinCEN's 2009 report Filing Trends in Mortgage Loan Fraud, as well as the FBI's report on mortgage fraud and the Mortgage Bankers Association report on mortgage loan originations, point to possible factors, including improved methods for detecting possible mortgage loan fraud prior to loan disbursement, an increase in criminal cases involving mortgage loan fraud, and a reduction in the availability of new Alt-A mortgage loans.

Financial Crimes Enforcement Network

U.S. Department of the Treasury

FinCEN is committed to distributing information to the public, financial industry professionals, and law enforcement professionals, in ways that can be readily found and used. We encourage feedback from readers on what information is of the greatest use. Your feedback is important and will assist us in planning future issues of FinCEN strategic analytical products. Please feel free to use this form, or provide your comments in the manner most convenient for you. The form can be faxed to FinCEN at (703) 905-3526 or e-mailed to Olerequests@fincen.gov.

Please identify your type of financial institution.

Depository Institution:

__ Bank or Bank Holding Company

__ Savings Association

__ Credit Union

__ Edge & Agreement Corporation

__ Foreign Bank with U.S. Branches or Agencies

Securities and Futures Industry:

__ Securities Broker/Dealer

__Futures Commission Merchant

__Introducing Broker in Commodities

__Mutual Fund

Money Services Business:

__ Money Transmitter

__ Money Order Company or Agent

__ Traveler's Check Company or Agent

__ Currency Dealer or Exchanger

__ U.S. Postal Service __ Stored Value

Casino or Card Club:

__ Casino located in Nevada

__ Casino located outside of Nevada

__ Card Club

__ **Insurance Company**

__**Dealers in Precious Metals, Precious Stones or Jewels**

__**Other** (please identify): _____

Please identify your Federal or State regulatory agency

__Federal Deposit Insurance Corporation

__Federal Reserve Board

__National Credit Union Administration

__Office of the Comptroller of the Currency

__Office of Thrift Supervision

__Securities & Exchange Commission

__State Regulatory Agency – please identify_____

__Other Federal Regulatory Agency– please identify:_____

Please identify your Federal, State or Local Law Enforcement Agency:

_____

Please identify other Federal, State or Local agency:_____

What information in this report did you find the most helpful or interesting? Please explain why:

_____
_____
_____
_____
_____

What information did you find least helpful or interesting? Please explain why:

_____

_____

_____

_____

_____

What new topics, trends, or patterns in suspicious activity would you like to see addressed in future FinCEN analytical reports? Please be specific - Examples might include: in a particular geographic area; concerning a certain type of transaction or instrument; other hot topics, etc.

_____

_____

_____

_____

_____

_____

Other Comments?:

_____

_____

Please email Feedback Forms to:
Olerequests@fincen.gov.

Or fax to:
Financial Crimes Enforcement Network (FinCEN)
(703) 905-3526

Or mail to:
FinCEN
P.O. Box 39
Vienna, VA 22183

www.FinCEN.gov